WE GO ECO

THE THINGS WE RECYCLE

WRITTEN BY KATIE WOOLLEY

ILLUSTRATED BY SOPHIE FOSTER

AND HANNAH WOOD

WINDMILL BOOKS

Published in 2027 by Windmill Books,
an Imprint of Rosen Publishing
2544 Clinton St.
Buffalo, NY 14224

First published in Great Britain in 2023 by Hodder and Stoughton

Illustrators: Sophie Foster and Hannah Wood
Design: Lisa Peacock
In-House Editor: Melanie Palmer

Picture credits:
p29 Robbert Frank Hagens/Alamy.

Cataloging-in-Publication Data
Names: Woolley, Katie, author. | Foster, Sophie, illustrator.
Title: The things we recycle / by Katie Woolley, illustrated by Sophie Foster.
Description: Buffalo, NY : Windmill Books, an imprint of Rosen Publishing, 2027. |
Series: We go eco | Includes glossary and index.
Identifiers: ISBN 9781725398481 (pbk.) | ISBN 9781725398498 (library bound) | ISBN 9781725398504 (ebook)
Subjects: LCSH: Recycling (Waste, etc.)--Juvenile literature. | Waste minimization--Juvenile literature. |
Environmental protection--Citizen participation--Juvenile literature.
Classification: LCC TD794.5 W66 2027 | DDC 363.728--dc23

Printed in China

CPSIA Compliance Information: Batch #QS27WM
For Further Information contact Rosen Publishing at 1-800-237-9932

CONTENTS

A LOT OF GARBAGE!

People make a lot of trash. When something is thrown away, it often gets sent to a landfill. However, we are running out of spaces to put our garbage.

Some trash can take years to break down. A plastic toothbrush takes 500 years to break down!

When food and natural materials end up in landfills, they rot. This releases harmful gases that contribute to global warming and climate change.

To help the planet...

WHAT IS RECYCLING?

Recycling means making trash into something new. Today, lots of things can be recycled. It is possible for some materials to be used and recycled more than once.

- Some plastic can be made into clothes, such as leggings and tops.

- Fishing nets can be turned into children's toys and games.

- Some plastic can be turned into furniture.

- Rugs can be made from recycled wool.

Today, more people want to help the planet. They want to recycle more things.

HOW ARE THINGS RECYCLED?

Different materials need to be recycled in different ways. It is important to find out how a material can be recycled safely.

- Glass and metal can be melted down and made into something new.

- Oil can get into rivers and seas and harm wildlife. It must be taken to a special place where it can be turned into new products.

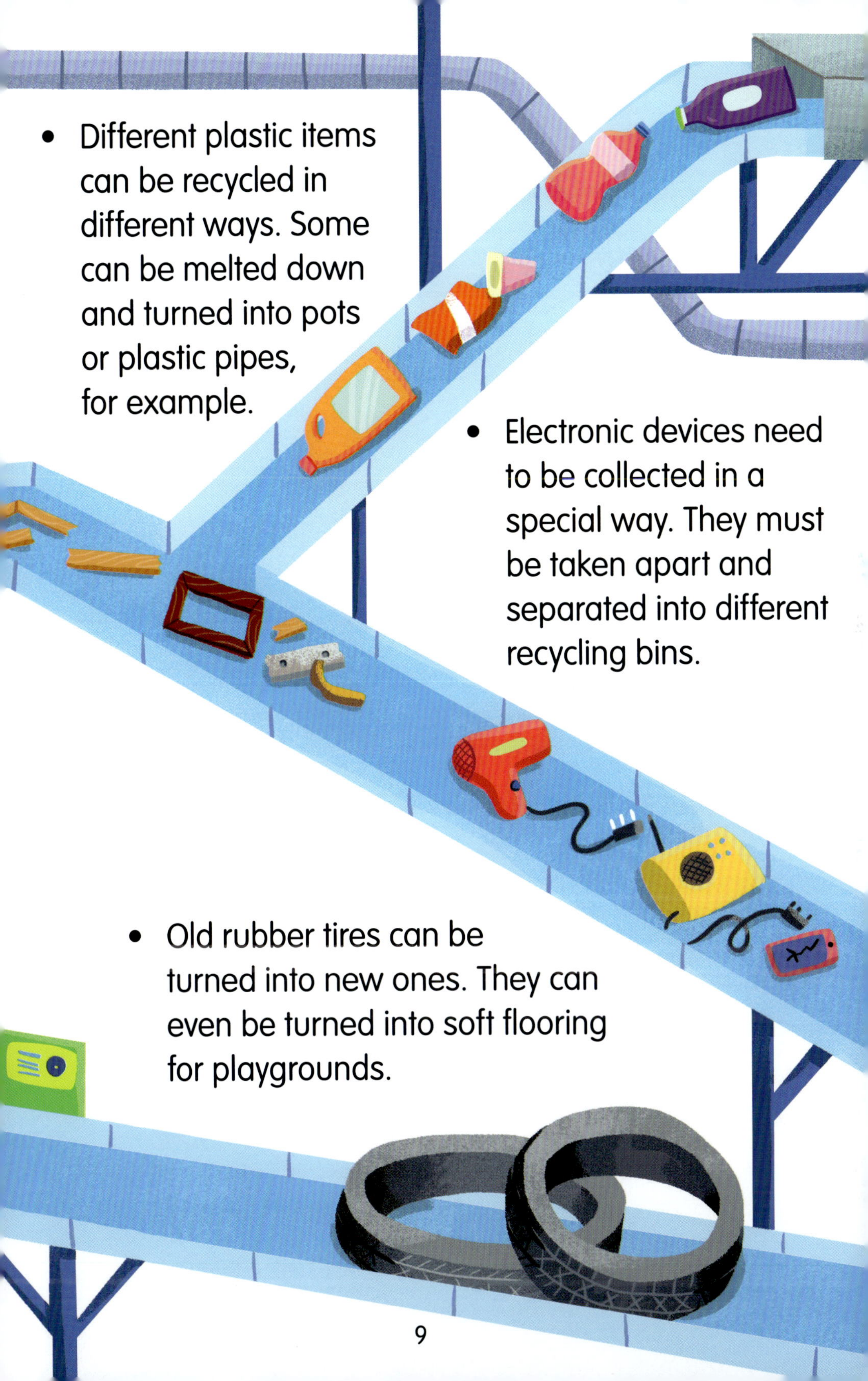

- Different plastic items can be recycled in different ways. Some can be melted down and turned into pots or plastic pipes, for example.
- Electronic devices need to be collected in a special way. They must be taken apart and separated into different recycling bins.
- Old rubber tires can be turned into new ones. They can even be turned into soft flooring for playgrounds.

PAPER

We use a lot of paper every day. We use it at school, at work, and at home.

- The bad news is that we cut down a lot of trees to make paper.
- The good news is that we are recycling more paper!

1. Used paper is sent to the paper mill.

2. Inside big machines called pulpers, the paper is mixed with water and chemicals. This washes away ink.

3. The paper is now called pulp.

4. The pulp is pushed between two wire mesh sheets to make a sheet of wet paper and left to dry.

5. The recycled paper is polished and rolled up, ready to send out.

Eco-Tip
An elephant makes enough poop every day to be turned into about 125 sheets of paper!

You can even make paper from elephant poop. The poop is collected and boiled. Then it is shaped into sheets of paper.

GLASS

Recycling glass is one of the ways we can reduce the amount of trash that ends up in landfills. Millions of tons of glass are recycled every year. But it is only a fraction of the glass that is made in one year.

3. The glass is sorted and taken to a glass treatment plant.

2. A truck takes our recycling to a recycling center.

1. At home, we put glass bottles and jars in our recycling bin.

Eco-Tip
Wash out bottles and jars before you put them in the recycling bin.

4. It is cleaned and sorted into colors.

5. Then it is crushed and melted.

6. The melted glass is made into new products, such as new bottles and jars.

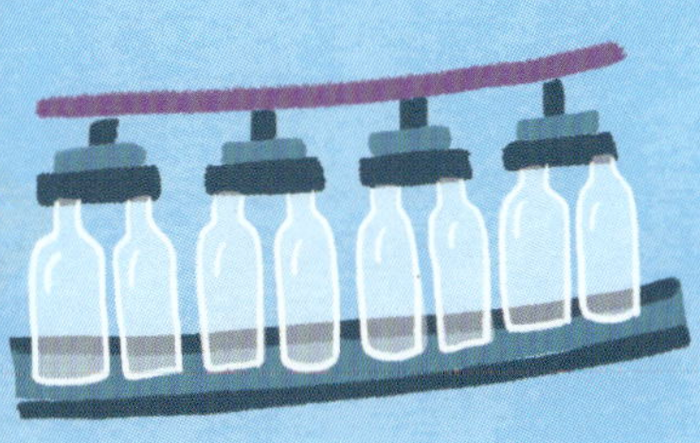

METAL

Hundreds of millions of tons of metal are recycled every year. The metal we throw away needs to be sorted into two groups: ferrous and non-ferrous metal.

A ferrous metal will be attracted to a magnet, but a non-ferrous metal won't.

non-ferrous metals: aluminium, lead, tin, copper, and gold

ferrous metals: iron, steel, and carbon steel (found in cars, fridges, and ovens)

Both types of metal can be recycled. Aluminium, steel, brass, and copper can be made into new things. Some parts of a car can be made from recycled metal.

Metal can be melted down and formed into new things, such as tables and airplane doors!

PLASTIC

Plastic is one of the biggest problems for our planet. A lot of plastic is used only once. This is called single-use plastic.

Plastic is often used in food packaging, and some toys and containers are made from it too.

Plastic can be useful. A helmet is made from plastic. It protects your head when you ride your bike.

Some medical machines have been built out of plastic. These machines save lives.

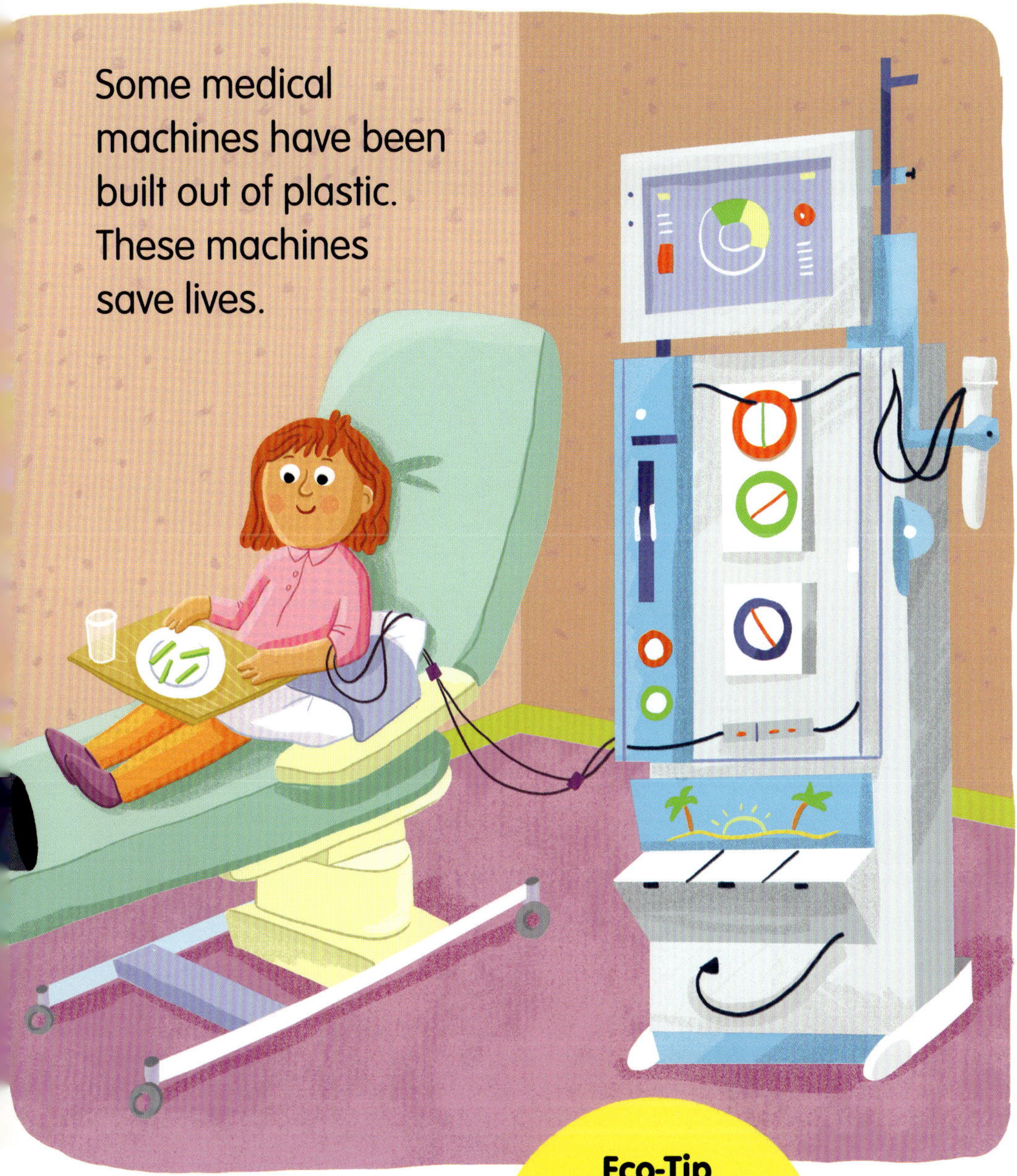

A cucumber wrapped in plastic lasts more than three times as long as an unwrapped one!

Eco-Tip

Use cloth shopping bags that can be reused, rather than plastic bags that get thrown away after one use.

PLASTIC IN THE WILD

Some plastic that is thrown away ends up in our oceans and harms Earth's wildlife. It can get wrapped around an animal's body or it can be mistaken for food and eaten.

In some countries, plastic garbage is left out on the streets to rot. In Indonesia, there is a system that helps people buy refills for products at a very low price. This means people are more likely to keep and reuse a plastic container.

People can pay to refill their containers with soap and shampoo.

CLOTHES AND TOYS

Take a look around your bedroom. Can you see any clothes or toys? Some are made from materials that can be recycled.

You can reuse old clothes and toys too. If you no longer wear something, or play with a toy, give it to a younger child or take it to a donation center.

You can turn old clothes into new ones. If your jeans are too short, cut off the bottoms to make some shorts!

UPCYCLING

Upcycling is a great way to reuse things you don't want to throw away. Lots of things can be upcycled. You just need to be a little bit creative!

You could give your upcycled objects to family and friends as gifts!

Upcycling reduces the amount of waste in landfill.

Eco-Tip
Try making art from some old garbage. What will you create?

Upcycling protects wildlife from waste and pollution.

It saves you money.

It inspires artists!

Belgian artist Wim Delvoye turns old objects into works of art. For one collection, he cut flowers and patterns into old tires. It looked like the patterns were carved from wood.

WHAT CAN WE DO AT HOME?

Here are some tips to Go Eco at home.

Get color-coded bins to make recycling easy for everyone. Most packaging has logos to help us figure out if it can be recycled or not.

Use a refillable cup.

Get crafty – reuse paper, plastic, and cardboard packaging.

Go digital. The more you do online, the less paper you will need.

Get a plastic-free toothbrush. Try a bamboo one!

Say NO to plastic straws.

ECO-TIP

Have a recycling competition with your friends. Make a reward chart to see who can recycle the most in a week!

Make a compost heap and add worms. They are nature's recyclers! They eat waste and turn it into compost that you can put on your garden.

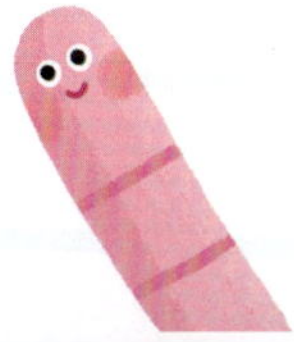

BECOME AN ECO WARRIOR

Talk to people about the planet and climate change. Tell them how recycling can help protect planet Earth.

Hold a clothes swap at school to reuse clothes.

Upcycle plastic containers. You could grow plants in yogurt containers or egg cartons!

Make posters that tell people about recycling.

Eco-Tip
Put your posters up around your school, or even your local town!

Encourage your school to commit to zero waste. This means having no food waste after lunch. It can be composted instead!

EARTH ACTIVIST: LILLY PLATT

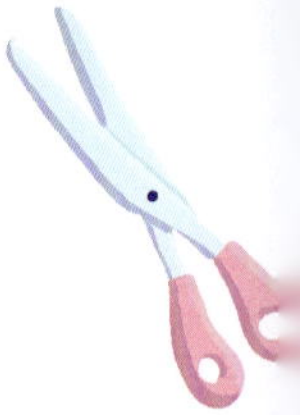

When Lilly Platt was young, her grandfather helped her learn her numbers by collecting and counting the plastic trash they found on the street.

Today, Lilly still picks up plastic waste and speaks out all around the world about the problem of plastic.

Lilly Platt (right, below) speaking out about plastic waste

GLOSSARY

Activist a person who takes action to make a change or to stop something from happening

Climate change the long-term changes in Earth's temperature and weather patterns

Compost nutrient-rich material made from rotting grass, leaves, and food

Ferrous metal a metal that contains iron, such as steel

Global warming the rising of the average temperature on Earth

Harm hurt

Landfill a piece of land where trash is taken after it is thrown away

Material the substance used to make something

Non-ferrous metal a metal that doesn't contain iron, such as aluminium, copper, tin, gold, and silver

Pollution when gases, smoke, or other harmful materials are released into the air, water, or land, causing harm to people, plants, and animals

Recycling the action of turning waste into something else that can be used

Upcycling taking something we would normally throw away and turning it into something useful

Zero waste a way of living in which we try to reduce the amount of trash we throw away

INDEX